"What I'd like to do is to go down in history as the president that made Americans believe in themselves again."

\- RONALD REAGAN

When the Reagan Library was dedicated in 1991, it was the President's dream that this institution would serve as an inspiration to young people. That it would be a place where they might learn from his leadership and share his vision - a timeless vision of hope and optimism for America and his belief that our best days lie ahead of us.

I was privileged to work in President Reagan's White House where I was inspired by his genuine civility and respect. While, yes, he held deep core beliefs, he fought hard and did his utmost to defeat his opponents, but never to destroy them.

At the end of the day, he showed that political adversaries could negotiate in an atmosphere of good will and mutual respect. And the nation was all the better because of that.

Today, this beautiful Library tells the story of President Reagan's dream; to learn about the awesome responsibilities of the executive office, distinctly unique and distinctly American; and to understand President Reagan's belief that we have a responsibility not only to preserve our own freedom, but to nurture it where it does not exist.

At the Reagan Library, visitors will learn about the challenges to our democratic way of life and how President Reagan faced them with steadfast fortitude and determination, while sharing faith in the boundless possibilities of America. It is our hope, as it was the President's, that bright young minds will come away from their experience with not only a sense of what was done in his time, but what they can do in theirs.

Fred. Ryan

Frederick J. Ryan
Chairman of the Board of Trustees

On November 4, 1991, an historic gathering of five presidents—Ronald Reagan, Richard Nixon, Gerald Ford, Jimmy Carter, and George H. W. Bush—celebrated the dedication of the Ronald Reagan Presidential Library and Museum. "The doors of this Library are open now and all are welcome," declared President Reagan. "The judgment of history is left to you, the people. I have no fears of that, for we have done our best. And so I say, come and learn from it."

On a hilltop in Simi Valley, the 153,000-square-foot Library is built in Spanish mission-style architecture. Paid for entirely by private donations, the structure has undergone a few significant changes since its opening in 1991. By adding the Air Force One Pavilion in 2005 to display the remarkable Boeing 707 aircraft, it became the only presidential library of its kind to feature such an airplane. In 2011, the Library honored the Ronald Reagan Centennial by updating and renovating the original museum galleries.

Even before the opening of the Air Force One Pavilion, the Reagan Library became hallowed ground in June 2004 as the final ceremony of President Reagan's funeral service was conducted here. His memorial site displays a quote from his speech delivered at the Library dedication in 1991 that captures the essence of his faith in human nature: "I know in my heart that man is good, that what is right will always eventually triumph and there is purpose and worth to each and every life."

The Library is made up of two distinct parts with separate but complementary missions. The first part is the museum with its permanent exhibit galleries and the special temporary exhibit space. The permanent exhibit tells the story of President Reagan's American journey from his childhood on the banks of the Rock River in Illinois to this glorious site overlooking the Pacific Ocean. Among others, the exhibit includes an exact reproduction of the Oval Office, a piece of the Berlin Wall, his mother's Bible held by Mrs. Reagan at his inaugurations, several interactive displays, and gifts from around the world.

The second part of the Library is the archive, which consists of the work product of the White House as well as materials relating to the life and political career of Ronald Reagan. The mission of the archival staff, under the leadership of the National Archives and Records Administration, is to arrange, preserve, and make available for research the approximately sixty million pages of documents, 1.6 million photographs, tens of thousands of audio and video tapes, and over 62,000 artifacts. While the vast majority of the records pertain to Ronald Reagan's two terms as president of the United States, the Library's archives also include materials relating to his two terms as governor of California as well as other pre- and post-presidential records.

Above all, the legacy of President Reagan and his life's work are preserved in the walls of his presidential library, which he dearly loved. "The journey has not just been my own," the fortieth president told us at the groundbreaking ceremony in 1988. He continued, "It seems I've been guided by a force much larger than myself, a force made up of ideas and beliefs about what this country is and what it could be."

On November 21, 1988, Ronald and Nancy Reagan turned the first shovels of earth on a windswept hill that began the realization of their shared vision to create a presidential library and museum that would preserve the achievements of President Reagan's enduring legacy of freedom.

On November 4, 1991, former president Ronald Reagan witnessed the largest gathering of past American presidents yet assembled for the dedication of this presidential library. One after another, they expressed their affection and admiration for the former leader.

George H. W. Bush: "As president, Ronald Reagan was unmoved by the vagaries of intellectual fashion. He treasured values that last, values that endure, and I speak of patriotism and civility and generosity and kindness, values etched in the American character."

Jimmy Carter: "Under President Ronald Reagan, our nation stood strong and resolute and made possible the beginning of the end of the Cold War. This has led to a new opportunity for our country, to exhibit its greatness which we accept for granted too often, more clearly to people around the world."

Gerald Ford: "President Reagan, you will be remembered as a national leader who was able to articulate the highest hopes and deepest beliefs of the American people. You have a great gift for transforming the best instincts into the firmest articles of faith; our misty memories of the past into bright visions of a better tomorrow."

Richard Nixon: "He believed in the simple things. He believed in freedom and democracy. He believed that America was on the right side of history, standing with the forces of good against the forces of evil in the world. And some have dismissed him therefore as an ideologue. But Ronald Reagan has been justified by what has happened. History has justified his leadership and those strong beliefs."

In response, former president Reagan spoke: "My fondest hope is that Americans will travel the road extending forward from the arch of experience, never forgetting our heroic origins, never failing to seek divine guidance as we march boldly, bravely, into a future limited only by our capacity to dream."

"The doors of this Library are open now and all are welcome. The judgment of history is left to you, the people. I have no fears of that, for we have done our best. And so I say, come and learn from it."

-RONALD REAGAN,
AT THE OPENING OF THE RONALD REAGAN PRESIDENTIAL LIBRARY AND MUSEUM

"*Ever since Franklin Delano Roosevelt, presidents have built libraries and amidst the surroundings that have shaped their characters and molded their values, from West Branch, Iowa, to Simi Valley, California, these institutions reflect the genius of the American people for self-government. Within their walls are housed millions of records for scholarly interpretation along with thousands of objects that give both solid and symbolic substance to this nation's highest office and to the forty men who have occupied it since Washington took his oath. Like the office they commemorate, presidential libraries are living institutions.*"

-RONALD REAGAN, NOVEMBER 4, 1991

To create an authentic sculpture, artist Glenna Goodacre studied many hours of video and hundreds of photographs in order to capture President Reagan's stride. A second casting of "After the Ride" is on display at the National Cowboy and Western Heritage Museum in Oklahoma City, Oklahoma, where, in 1989, President Reagan was inducted into the Hall of Great Westerners. Deeply honored by such recognition, he accepted the award in person and expressed his admiration for Western culture and lifestyle.

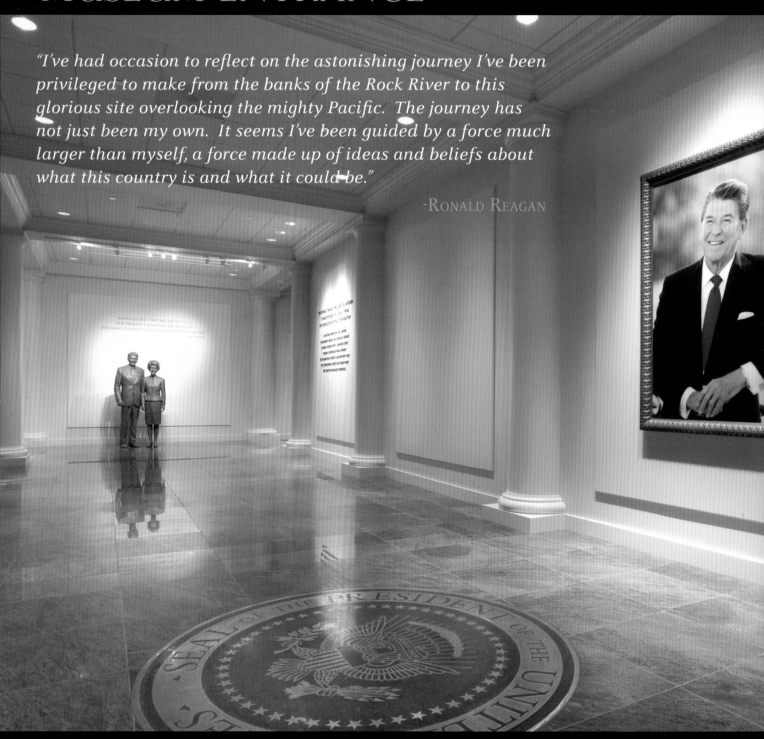

"I've had occasion to reflect on the astonishing journey I've been privileged to make from the banks of the Rock River to this glorious site overlooking the mighty Pacific. The journey has not just been my own. It seems I've been guided by a force much larger than myself, a force made up of ideas and beliefs about what this country is and what it could be."

-RONALD REAGAN

Ronald Reagan was one of the most influential leaders of the twentieth century. He led a profound change in our world—at home and abroad. His deep convictions, optimism, and determination continue to inspire millions of people around the world today.

"AMERICA'S BEST DAYS ARE YET TO COME.
OUR PROUDEST MOMENTS ARE YET TO BE.
OUR MOST GLORIOUS ACHIEVEMENTS ARE JUST AHEAD."

RONALD REAGAN

The life-sized bronze statues of Ronald and Nancy Reagan were sculpted by noted American artist Chas Fagan, who also created the statues of President Reagan that are displayed in the Capitol Rotunda in Washington, D.C., and in Grosvenor Square in London.

The Reagan Hologram: Working with award-winning Hollywood special effects masters and hologram innovators, the Reagan Library created a first-of-its-kind hologram of our nation's 40th President. Committed to the use of emerging technologies to share history, this experience is enthralling, engaging and educational.

> "I'm reminded of my parents' teachings...everything works out for the best and individuals determine their destiny through ambition and hard work."
>
> RONALD REAGAN

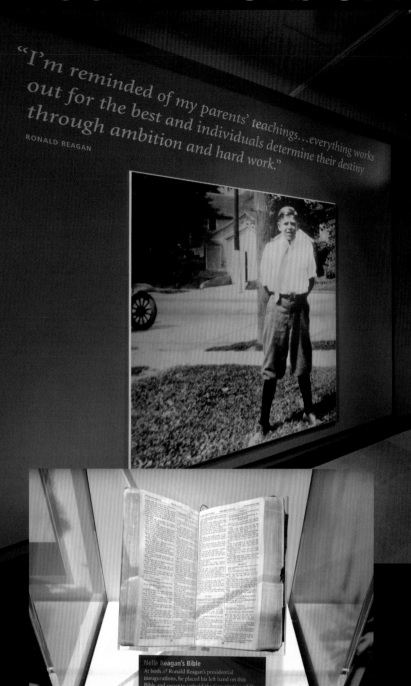

EVOLUTION OF A
GREAT COMMUNICATOR

Ronald Reagan's early life in rural Illinois reveals lessons, beliefs, and personal strengths that guided him for the rest of his life. Ronald Reagan's mother, Nelle, and his father, Jack, taught him the values of faith, fairness, optimism, and trust. The courage and values he showed as president were already visible in the young man.

Nelle Reagan's Bible
At both of Ronald Reagan's presidential inaugurations, he placed his left hand on this Bible and swore to uphold the Constitution of the United States. The Bible belonged to his mother and contains her handwritten notes inside.

A Bible is on display that belonged to Ronald Reagan's mother and was used in both inaugural ceremonies. An excerpt from a handwritten sonnet by Nelle Reagan closes with:

> "In thought of mind, in word, and in each deed
> My life must prove the power of His grace
> By every action through my living days."

Ronald Reagan immersed himself in life at college and he proved to be an accomplished athlete, actor, and leader. He sampled the full breadth of what education had to offer.

During these formative years, he was on the yearbook staff, elected to student government, a member of a fraternity, president of the drama club, and a regular cast member in school plays, in addition to his year-round athletics. He graduated from Eureka College with a bachelor's degree in economics.

The Foundations of the Great Communicator Gallery explores the development of Ronald Reagan as a speaker, leader, and politician of deep conviction. It begins with his first job as a radio announcer at WOC in Davenport, Iowa, which became the launching pad for his film career. As an announcer for the Chicago Cubs in 1937, he attended spring training on the Southern California coast. An old acquaintance in Los Angeles introduced him to an agent, who arranged a screen test. A few days later, he had a telegram offering him a contract with Warner Bros. Starring in over fifty films, the young Reagan answered the call to leadership by heading the Screen Actors Guild during difficult times when the motion picture industry was challenged by bitter labor disputes.

Left: Ronald Reagan on the set of GE Theater.

Below: Ronald Reagan's first radio job was broadcasting a University of Iowa football game for WOC Radio in Davenport, Iowa.

"Those GE tours became a post-graduate course in political science for me. I was seeing how government really worked and affected people in the grass roots of America, not how it was taught in school."

-RONALD REAGAN

It was also during this important period that he met and married actress Nancy Davis, who "enriched his life forever." Only a few years after their wedding, the young Reagan was offered an exceptional opportunity with GE in a dual role: as host of GE Theater and as goodwill ambassador. For eight years, he helped reinforce the links between headquarters and the sprawling company, visiting 139 factories in thirty-nine states. It was an invaluable apprenticeship in public speaking, political philosophy, and understanding the American people.

more

"Our problems are many but our capacity to solve them is limitless."

Announcing his candidacy for governor of California on January 4, 1966, with his wife Nancy at his side, he delivered a simple, consistent message advocating economic freedom, smaller government, fewer regulations, and lower taxes.

Defeating incumbent Pat Brown by a margin of 58 to 42 percent, Ronald Reagan was elected governor of California and inaugurated on January 2, 1967. The capabilities Ronald Reagan possessed from an early age—empathy, good instincts, and common sense—allowed him to flourish as governor.

The gallery documents his accomplishments in four key areas:

Reforming Welfare

California's welfare program was a huge burden on a financially strapped state, costing over $3 billion a year. Governor Reagan undertook a sweeping welfare reform plan, saving hundreds of millions of dollars.

Protecting the Environment

With an admirable record of safeguarding the environment, he added 145,000 acres of park land, enforced tougher measures on air and water quality, stopped plans for dams on two rivers, and despite intense pressure from commercial interests, signed into law a bill to protect California's wild and scenic rivers.

Cutting Taxes, Shrinking Government

Inheriting a state government with a deficit of over $200 million, Governor Reagan was forced to raise taxes, impose spending cuts, enforce a hiring freeze, and cancel projects. By 1968, California had a $100-million surplus and over a period of a few years, returned $5.7 billion in taxes to Californians.

Supporting Education

Putting a stop to the unrest on the state's college campuses was critical. As governor, he tightened the laws against unlawful assembly and suspended financial support of students convicted in campus disturbances. Spending for education was increased 89 percent during the Reagan Administration.

A Time for Choosing

In 1961, Senator Barry Goldwater (R-AZ) heard Ronald Reagan deliver a speech at the Phoenix Chamber of Commerce as part of GE's national outreach. An alliance developed between the two men and eventually Senator Goldwater asked the young Reagan to become California's manager for his 1964 presidential campaign. Hitting the campaign trail for Goldwater, Ronald Reagan developed a speech entitled "A Time for Choosing," which was ultimately delivered on national television on October 27, 1964. Sometimes referred to as the "Rendezvous with Destiny Speech," it vaulted him to prominence and established his ability as an inspirational speaker and man of conservative ideas.

"Americans... were trying to cope with the ruthless effects of double-digit inflation, which was eating away at their savings, their paychecks, and their way of life..."

-RONALD REAGAN

On top of the political turmoil of the decade, Americans suffered from a stagnant economy and high inflation at the same time. This "stagflation" made homes, food, energy, and other goods steadily more expensive as jobs disappeared.

As one measure of the economy, an economist created the "Misery Index," the unemployment rate and inflation rate combined. During the 1970s, the index more than doubled to its highest point ever, almost 22 percent. Many Americans began to lose faith in the American Dream.

The U.S. military retreated from South Vietnam. A bungled burglary unraveled into the Watergate affair and the resignation of President Richard Nixon. Some Americans began to fear that their government and military were inept; or worse, dishonorable.

At home, Americans suffered through factory closures, high energy prices, gas lines, and a ten-year battle with inflation. In 1979, the Soviet Union brutally invaded Afghanistan, and Iranian radicals took sixty-six Americans hostage.

The Geographical Election of
Ronald Reagan in 1980

Ronald Reagan announced his candidacy for the presidency on November 13, 1979. Over the next eight months, he surged ahead of other Republican candidates to win the GOP nomination.

Ronald Reagan's campaign, victory, and inauguration marked a profound change in American politics. On the campaign trail, he offered a new direction for the country. From the first day of his presidency, he began to implement his core philosophy of smaller government, lower taxes, and a strong national defense. And he continued his crusade to help Americans believe in themselves again.

"More than anything else, I want my candidacy to unify our country; to renew the American spirit and sense of purpose."

-RONALD REAGAN

VICTORY AND INAUGURATION

A selection of President Reagan's inaugural address speech cards, January 20, 1981, on display in this gallery.

Deliver President Reagan's inaugural address at the podium in the gallery.

"Let us begin an era of national renewal. Let us renew our determination, our courage, and our strength. And let us renew our faith and our hope. We have every right to dream heroic dreams."

-RONALD REAGAN, INAUGURAL ADDRESS, JANUARY 20, 1981

The Victory and Inauguration Gallery tells the story of Ronald Reagan's election victory which marked a profound change in American politics. Carrying forty-four of fifty states in 1980, he attracted votes from many Democrats and Independents. He led Republicans to control of the U.S. Senate for the first time in twenty-eight years, though Democrats still controlled the House of Representatives and would challenge many of his ideas throughout his presidency.

The election of 1980 marked the beginning of the "Reagan Revolution" based on freedom, economic opportunity, national pride, and global democracy.

The other story told in this gallery documents how President Reagan began putting his ideas about government and the economy into practice during the first seventy days in office.

A GREATER PURPOSE

"Perhaps having come so close to death made me feel I should do whatever I could in the years God had given me to reduce the threat of nuclear war."

-RONALD REAGAN

Step into history. The date is March 30, 1981. President Ronald Reagan has just delivered an important economic speech at the Washington Hilton Hotel and walks outside about 2:25 p.m. An assassin's shot rings out. The immersive experience in this gallery personifies the intensity of this terrifying event.

President Reagan's personal courage and determination to reassure the American people despite his pain transformed this horrifying act of violence into an inspirational story. Despite losing almost half his blood volume after the attack, President Reagan's humor emerged as they wheeled him into surgery: "I hope you're all Republicans," he said. During his recovery, he reached out to Soviet General Secretary Leonid Brezhnev by composing a handwritten letter on a legal pad, displayed in the gallery.

At the hospital and later the White House, he received an outpouring of good wishes from the nation in cards, gifts, and prayers. His humor and good spirits helped give the nation hope. And he came to believe his life had been spared for a reason, to continue his work toward peace.

With Mrs. Reagan and their daughter Patti at his side, President Reagan left George Washington University Hospital on April 11, 1981.

President Reagan remained in George Washington University Hospital for twelve days. The president's strong will and remarkable vitality helped him make a speedy recovery. The assassination attempt was an agonizing ordeal for President and Mrs. Reagan, the other men wounded in the attack, and their families. It was a trial for the American people and finally a story of courage, reassurance, and inspiration as President Reagan returned to the White House.

"What happens now, I owe my life to God and will try to serve Him every way I can."

-RONALD REAGAN, DIARY, APRIL 1981

Above: Official 1985 White House portrait of President Ronald Wilson Reagan.

The Oval Office symbolizes the power, prestige, and solemn responsibilities of the presidency. In addition to a working office, the historic space is where presidents welcome foreign dignitaries and special guests. As dictated by custom, each new president completely decorates the office to suit his individual taste and preferences. President Reagan's love of the West and relaxed style is reflected in the Remington bronzes, Western paintings, and the obligatory jar of Jelly Belly jelly beans.

"If we're to continue to advance world peace and human freedom, America must remain strong.... Peace through Strength works."

—RONALD REAGAN, SEPTEMBER 24, 1988

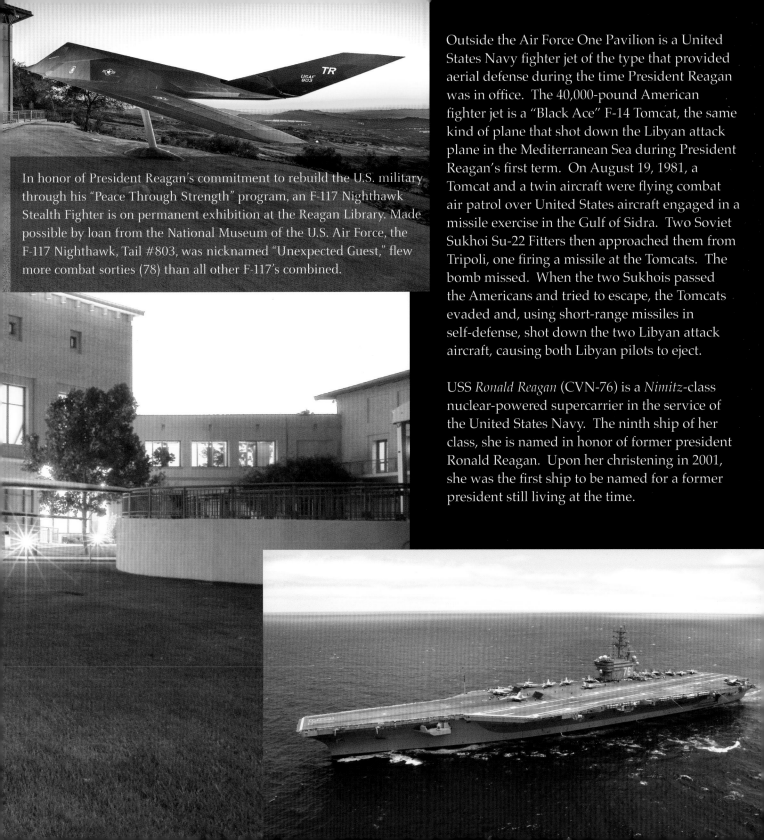

In honor of President Reagan's commitment to rebuild the U.S. military through his "Peace Through Strength" program, an F-117 Nighthawk Stealth Fighter is on permanent exhibition at the Reagan Library. Made possible by loan from the National Museum of the U.S. Air Force, the F-117 Nighthawk, Tail #803, was nicknamed "Unexpected Guest," flew more combat sorties (78) than all other F-117's combined.

Outside the Air Force One Pavilion is a United States Navy fighter jet of the type that provided aerial defense during the time President Reagan was in office. The 40,000-pound American fighter jet is a "Black Ace" F-14 Tomcat, the same kind of plane that shot down the Libyan attack plane in the Mediterranean Sea during President Reagan's first term. On August 19, 1981, a Tomcat and a twin aircraft were flying combat air patrol over United States aircraft engaged in a missile exercise in the Gulf of Sidra. Two Soviet Sukhoi Su-22 Fitters then approached them from Tripoli, one firing a missile at the Tomcats. The bomb missed. When the two Sukhois passed the Americans and tried to escape, the Tomcats evaded and, using short-range missiles in self-defense, shot down the two Libyan attack aircraft, causing both Libyan pilots to eject.

USS *Ronald Reagan* (CVN-76) is a *Nimitz*-class nuclear-powered supercarrier in the service of the United States Navy. The ninth ship of her class, she is named in honor of former president Ronald Reagan. Upon her christening in 2001, she was the first ship to be named for a former president still living at the time.

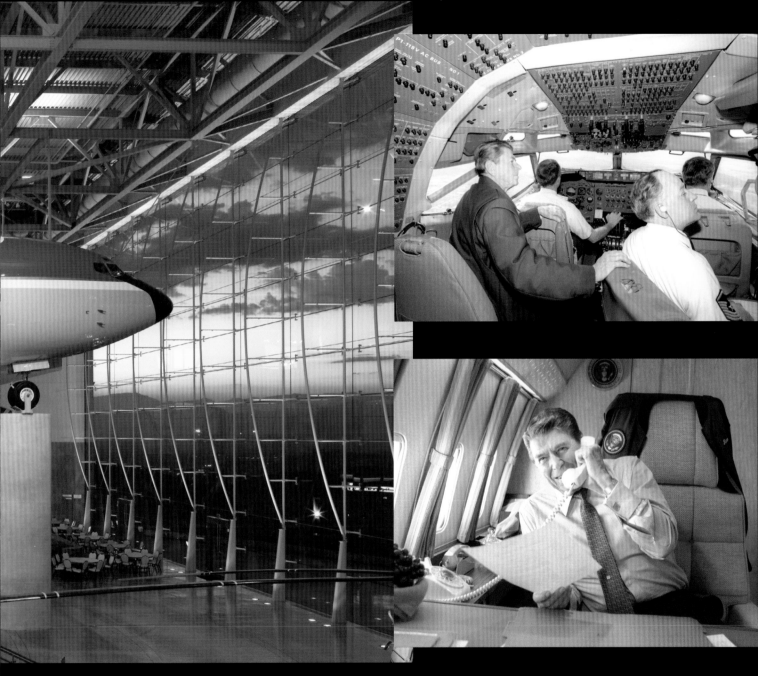

Visitors have the unique opportunity to walk through Air Force One and view each compartment from the flight deck to the communications center, the presidential cabin, the conference room, and the galleys. Almost fully restored, each area is detailed in the era of Ronald Reagan's presidency aboard America's Flying White House.

This is the last Boeing 707 to see presidential service and one that accumulated an impressive record of twenty-eight years flying seven presidents on 445 missions, 1,440 sorties, and covering 1,314,596 miles of air travel. Nearly half of the missions—211 domestic and international—were with President Reagan, who flew aboard this aircraft more miles than any other president. In all, there were fifty international missions visiting more than 200 cities worldwide during President Reagan's eight years in the White House.

A presidential motorcade is featured beneath the wings of Air Force One including President Reagan's 1984 armored Cadillac limousine, a 1986 Secret Service Chevrolet Suburban chase vehicle, a 1982 Los Angeles Police Department patrol car, and two 1980s Los Angeles Police Department motorcycles.

The actual Ronald Reagan Pub, which President and Mrs. Reagan visited in Ballyporeen, Ireland in 1984, was moved to the Reagan Library in 2005. The Ronald Reagan Pub now resides in our Air Force One Pavilion.

The Air Force One Pavilion houses a Sikorsky VH-3 Sea King helicopter with the call sign "Marine One."

"Welcome here to your house, which you're letting me live in for a while."

The Executive Mansion located at 1600 Pennsylvania Avenue in Washington, D.C., is a symbol above all else of the great power and responsibility of the president of the United States. But it is also an office building, tourist destination, landmark, national stage, and performance venue, as well as a home, retreat, and the headquarters of the leader of the free world.

President and Mrs. Reagan loved celebrating birthdays, anniversaries, and other family events in the White House. But presidents and first ladies also honor the nation's customs and traditions by leading the celebration of holidays from the Fourth of July to Christmas and Hanukkah.

Over eight years, Ronald Reagan kept a daily diary in which he recorded his thoughts on the extraordinary, the historic, and the routine day-to-day occurrences of his presidency. In this gallery, President Reagan's handwritten diary is on display showing the daily entries he recorded at his desk in the White House. To give the visitor the opportunity to explore these historic volumes, an interactive diary experience has been created.

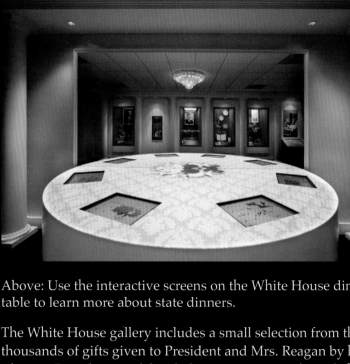

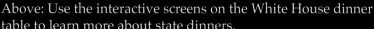

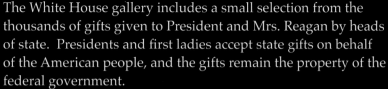

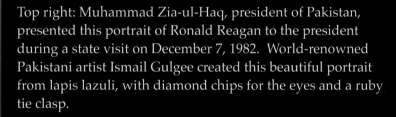

Above: Use the interactive screens on the White House dinner table to learn more about state dinners.

The White House gallery includes a small selection from the thousands of gifts given to President and Mrs. Reagan by heads of state. Presidents and first ladies accept state gifts on behalf of the American people, and the gifts remain the property of the federal government.

Top right: Muhammad Zia-ul-Haq, president of Pakistan, presented this portrait of Ronald Reagan to the president during a state visit on December 7, 1982. World-renowned Pakistani artist Ismail Gulgee created this beautiful portrait from lapis lazuli, with diamond chips for the eyes and a ruby tie clasp.

Middle right: This elephant figure made of rosewood inlaid with silver and semiprecious stones was a gift from Hema Premadasa, wife of the prime minister of Sri Lanka, in 1985.

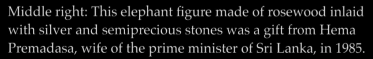

Above: This Sèvres ceramic sculpture was a gift from Danielle Mitterrand, first lady of France, in July 1986, in conjunction with the one-hundredth anniversary of the Statue of Liberty.

Left: President and Mrs. Reagan greet Prime Minister Margaret and Mr. Denis Thatcher of the United Kingdom for the final state dinner at the North Portico of the White House, November 16, 1988.

THE FIRST LADY

"Ronnie and I were privileged to have an opportunity given to a very few—to be a part of history and the shaping of it."

– NANCY REAGAN

The First Lady's Gallery honors not only her life and accomplishments, but also tells the heartwarming story of her marriage to Ronald Reagan. From her childhood to the breadth of her acting career to the beginning of an historic love story, the story of Nancy Davis emerges.

After eight years as California's first lady from 1967 to 1974, Nancy Reagan's life in the political arena had just begun. Seven years later, in 1981, Nancy Davis Reagan became the nation's hostess, the social director of the White House, and an international ambassador when her husband became America's fortieth president. Like other first ladies, she was also the president's closest confidante and staunchest defender. Taking her responsibility seriously, she represented the country with grace and dignity, whether entertaining heads of state in the White House, promoting her "Just Say No" anti-drug campaign, or working with the Foster Grandparents Program.

Visitors to the First Lady's Gallery will learn more about Mrs. Reagan's "Just Say No" campaign, for which she traveled over 250,000 miles across the United States and foreign countries to fight substance abuse. By 1988, more than 12,000 "Just Say No" clubs had been formed around the world.

When President and Mrs. Reagan moved into the White House in 1981, they discovered that portions of the White House and Blair House, the president's official guest house, badly needed restoration. Visitors to this gallery will learn how Mrs. Reagan led the effort to raise the necessary funds from private donors to preserve these national treasures.

After leaving the White House, her husband was diagnosed with Alzheimer's disease in 1994. Mrs. Reagan spoke in support of stem cell research, which promised new hope for patients with Alzheimer's and other illnesses.

Above: President and Mrs. Reagan on the White House South Lawn.

"I've said it before and I'll say it once again: my life didn't begin until I met Ronnie."

– NANCY REAGAN

Above: A few of the beautiful gowns worn by Nancy Reagan are displayed. Early in the Reagan Administration, the press criticized Nancy Reagan for perceived lavish expenses on china and in re-decorating the White House, as well as accepting donations and loans of gowns and other apparel, though no public funds were spent.

"Drugs take away the dream from every child's heart and replace it with a nightmare and it's time we in America stand up and replace those dreams."

- NANCY REAGAN

In the Terry Lanni Rose Garden at the Reagan Library, you'll discover a stunning bronze sculpture of our first lady, Nancy Reagan. Created by world-renowned sculptor Chas Fagan, she's seated on a bench, with a basket of two items. First, there are peonies, of course, her favorite flower. And secondly, there's a little piece of the Berlin wall folded up in a copy of the Washington Post. Remember, she whispered "peace" in the ear of Soviet Foreign Minister, Andrei Gromyko.

REBUILDING AMERICA

In 1980, America was in the throes of a full-blown recession, with sky-high interest rates, massive unemployment, and a pervasive air of gloom. When President Reagan took office, he set to work implementing his plan to rebuild America based on four objectives: cutting taxes, reducing government spending, eliminating excessive regulations, and tightening the monetary policy to curb inflation.

President Reagan fervently believed that lower tax rates would make the American people more industrious and more prosperous, and bring more revenue for the government. Some economists dubbed this principle "supply side economics." The president called it "common sense." This gallery is dedicated to telling the story of President Reagan's economic policy along with other important domestic issues like the Air Traffic Controllers' Strike of 1981, the Supreme Court nominations, the 1984 election, and the space shuttle Challenger tragedy.

"With my advisors I had begun working on an economic recovery plan the first day after the election. The morning after Inauguration Day, at our first cabinet meeting and a meeting the following day of a team of specialists I had appointed to coordinate economic policy, we began the job of implementing the plan. Its basis was tax reform: reducing federal income tax rates from top to bottom."

-RONALD REAGAN

Will I find a job?

Will our taxes keep increasing?

THE GRADUATE

Will I keep my job?

THE FACTORY WORKER

Can we afford a new home?

How can I find more customers?

Learn more about President Reagan's policies and ideas by playing the electronic interactive game "Rebuilding America," a focal point of the gallery.

THE BERLIN WALL AND THREAT THEATER

"It takes more than walls and guns to imprison the human spirit."

- RONALD REAGAN

As the United States grew more prosperous at home, it still faced the challenge of an expansionist, oppressive, totalitarian system abroad—international communism and, especially, the Soviet Union.

This gallery defines the complex world events preceding Ronald Reagan's election as America's fortieth president. It describes how the Iron Curtain took shape after World War II, not only as a divider, but also as an idea representing the profound division between communism and democracy, oppression and freedom.

Visitors will discover how the Soviet Union dominated the Eastern side of the Iron Curtain and enforced its brand of communism in its satellite states. Ronald Reagan took on the enormous challenge of reuniting Germany and bringing down the Iron Curtain. Artifacts on display reflect the brutal suppression inflicted by East German Border Guards and the Stasi (Secret Police) on innocent citizens.

Threat Theater is an immersive experience which documents the threat posed by communism. It explains the struggles between East and West during the Cold War era and introduces Ronald Reagan's thoughts on communism in the decades leading up to his presidency.

PEACE THROUGH STRENGTH

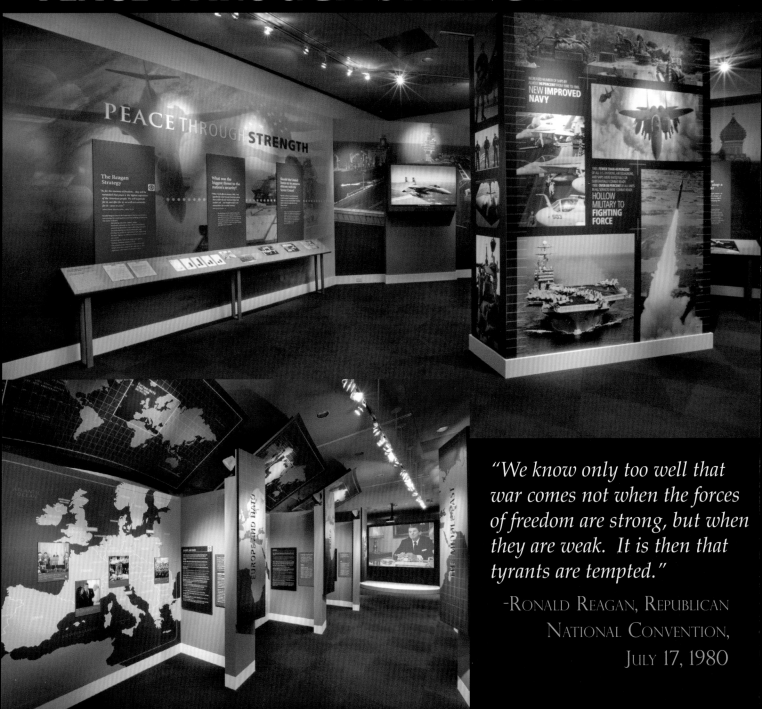

"We know only too well that war comes not when the forces of freedom are strong, but when they are weak. It is then that tyrants are tempted."

-RONALD REAGAN, REPUBLICAN NATIONAL CONVENTION, JULY 17, 1980

This gallery celebrates President Reagan's courage as a leader, skill as a diplomat, and his willingness to confront communism in order to end Soviet domination. He developed and applied with constant purpose a strategy not simply to contain communism, but to eliminate it, and he achieved this goal across much of the globe.

In 1981, Ronald Reagan entered the White House determined to restore the strength of the U.S. military. He insisted on military might not for its own sake, but to discourage threats to American interests, defend freedom around the world, and bring the Soviet Union to the bargaining table.

The F-117 Nighthawk, Tail Number 803 and produced by Lockheed Martin, is on display at the Reagan Library. Nicknamed, "Unexpected Guest," the aircraft served from 1984-2007 and flew the most combat sorties of all F-117's.

This M1 Abrams Main Battle Tank was dedicated at the Reagan Library on December 4, 2021. Designed as a highly mobile main-battle tank for modern armored ground warfare, it entered the Army's arsenal in 1980. Weighing in at 62 metric tons, it's one of the heaviest main battle tanks in service and was named after United States Army General Creighton Williams Abrams, Jr.

His strategy included:

• Rebuilding America's military

• Fearlessly pointing out the evils of communism, promoting democracy, and reaffirming America's moral leadership on the international stage

• Ending the policy of containment and supporting freedom fighters to roll back communism around the world

• Protecting the American people through the Strategic Defense Initiative (SDI)

• Reducing and eventually eliminating the threat of nuclear weapons through face-to-face diplomacy and improved communication

"As for the enemies of freedom… they will be reminded that peace is the highest aspiration of the American people. We will negotiate for it; sacrifice for it; we will not surrender for it—now or ever."

- RONALD REAGAN, INAUGURAL ADDRESS, JANUARY 20, 1981

"No foe of freedom should doubt our resolve. We will prevail because our faith is strong and our cause is just."

- RONALD REAGAN, FEBRUARY 26, 1981

VOICES OF FREEDOM

During his eight years in office, President Reagan reached out to leaders throughout the world. He encouraged them to fight for freedom wherever they found oppression and pledged the support of his administration to help win peace and democracy for all people.

"Survival in this era requires us, as those who preceded us, to take freedom in the palms of our hands and never to cower behind a veil of unrealistic optimism. We shall learn from those who spoke of the need for vigilance, even when speaking out was not popular."

- RONALD REAGAN

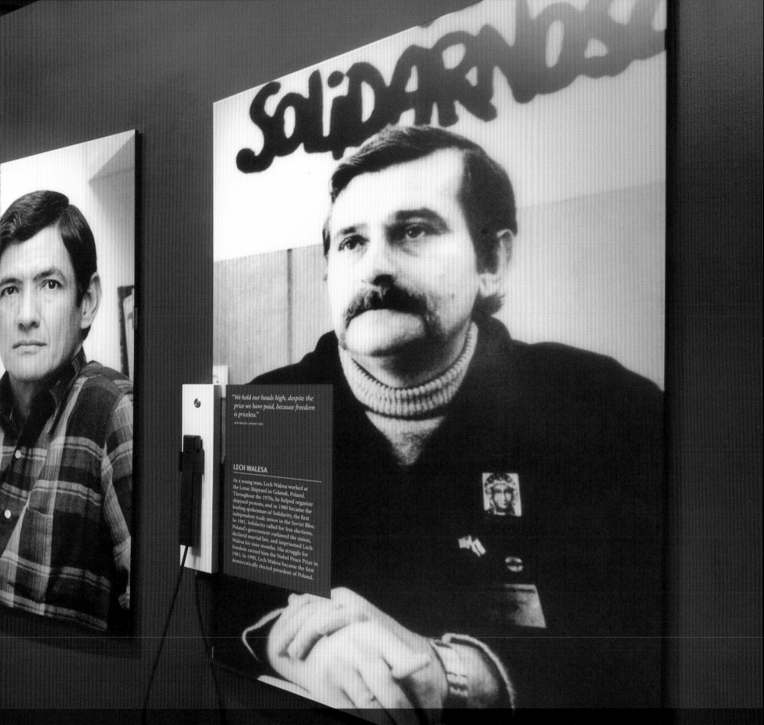

President Reagan's unshakable, lifelong opposition to communism and staunch support of human rights helped to free hundreds of millions of people around the globe. His "behind-the-scenes" diplomacy was crucial in securing permission for thousands of Soviet Jews to immigrate to Israel. But he also reached out to foreign leaders to secure freedom for individuals held as political prisoners. President Reagan's commitment echoes to this day in the voices of men and women seeking freedom around the world.

Ronald Reagan and Mikhail Gorbachev transformed relations between the United States and the Soviet Union at four major summits: Geneva, Switzerland; Reykjavik, Iceland; Washington, D.C.; and Moscow, U.S.S.R. Between November 1985 and May 1988, they signed two historic treaties, negotiated dramatic reductions in nuclear arms, and began to bring the Cold War to an end.

This gallery is dedicated to each of these four historic meetings, the difficult process of negotiation, and the ultimate outcome: the signing and ratification of the INF treaty which, for the first time ever, destroyed an entire class of nuclear weapons.

A video presentation documents the personal relationship that grew between Ronald Reagan and Mikhail Gorbachev which helped to change the world. At times, their negotiations erupted into open anger. Both men were ultimately bold enough to trust each other, or as President Reagan said repeatedly, "trust but verify."

At the close of the Moscow Summit in 1988, President Reagan and General Secretary Gorbachev issued a joint statement that "both nations were determined to prevent any war between them" and disavowed "an intention to achieve military superiority."

A year later, the Berlin Wall fell, the Soviet Union dissolved by 1991, and in ten years, the United States reduced its nuclear arsenals by 38 percent and in turn, Russia reduced theirs by 53 percent. After nearly five decades, the Cold War was over.

"And so, we will work together that we might forever keep our swords at our sides."

- RONALD REAGAN, MAY 28, 1988

"*Strengthened by their courage, heartened by their valor, and borne by their memory, let us continue to stand for the ideals for which they lived and died.*"

- RONALD REAGAN, JUNE 1984

We dedicate this gallery to all those men and women—military and civilian—who made the ultimate sacrifice in defense of our freedom and in service of our country. Ronald Reagan made a point of honoring American heroes. His State of the Union addresses began a tradition of extending the nation's gratitude to ordinary citizens who met extraordinary challenges. This gallery tells the stories of these and other such heroes from yesterday and today.

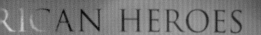

"*Those who say that we're in a time when there are no heroes—they just don't know where to look… Their patriotism is quiet, but deep. Their values sustain our national life. Now, I have used the words 'they' and 'their' in speaking of these heroes. I could say 'you' and 'your,' because I'm addressing the heroes of whom I speak: you, the citizens of this blessed land. Your dreams, your hopes, your goals are going to be the dreams, the hopes, and the goals of this administration, so help me God.*"

- RONALD REAGAN

Medal of Honor

President Ronald Reagan presented this Medal of Honor to Master Sergeant Roy Benavidez on February 24, 1981.

47

CAMP DAVID

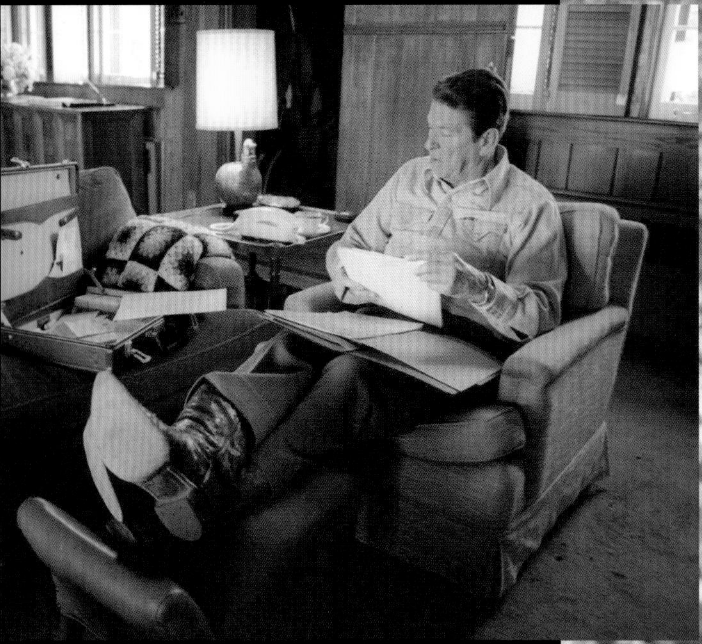

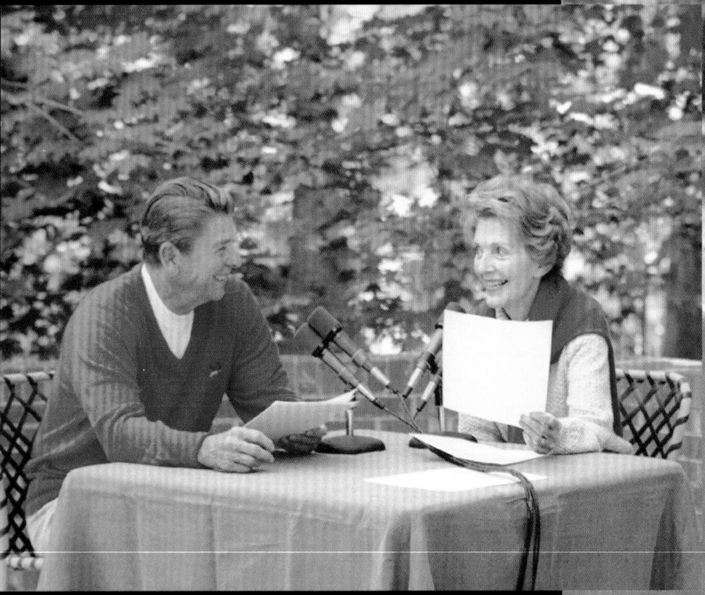

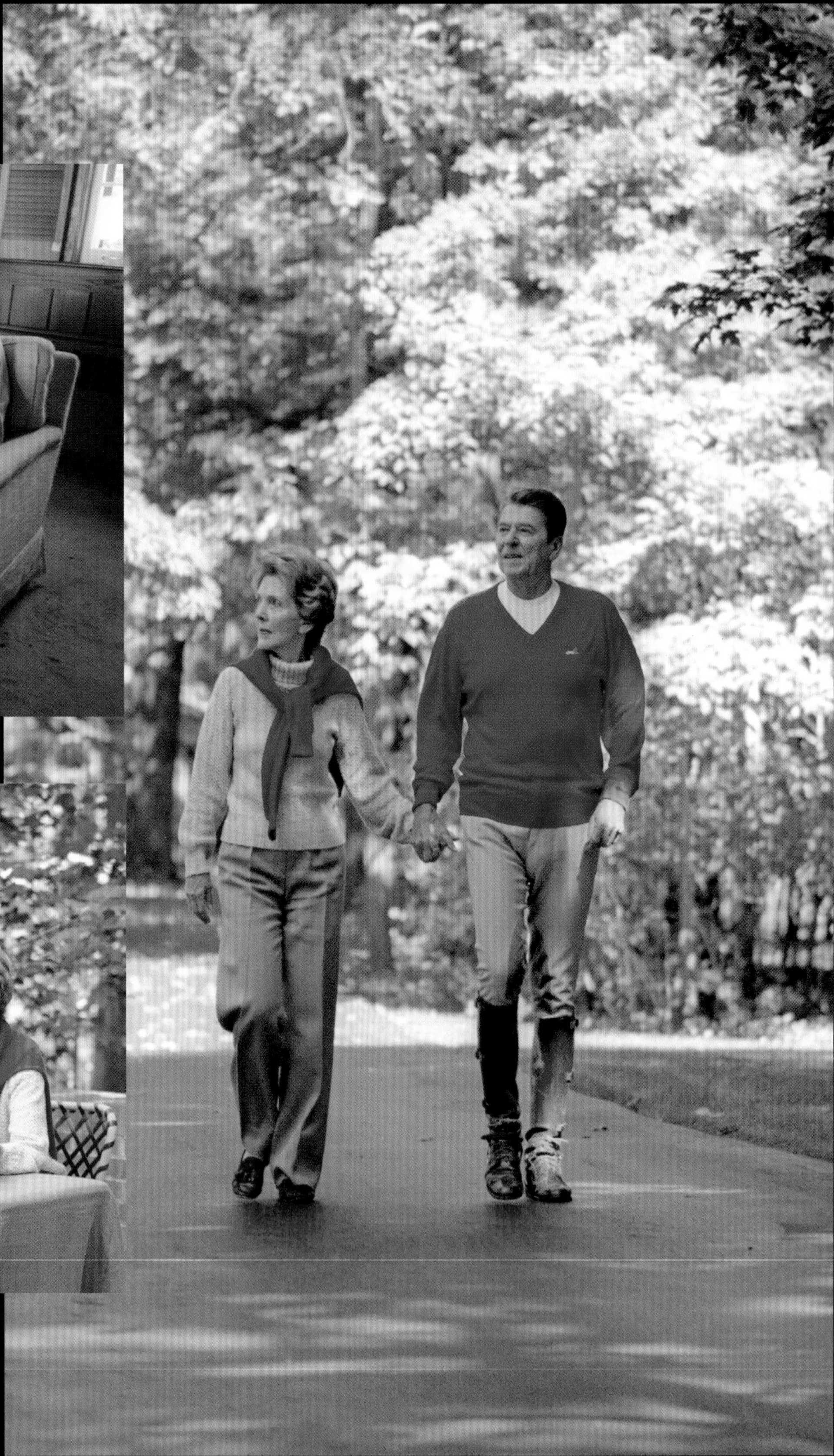

"I usually took a pile of homework and made my weekly radio broadcast during our weekends at Camp David."
- RONALD REAGAN

Camp David was another sanctuary for President and Mrs. Reagan. The camp is actually a small U.S. Navy installation in the Catoctin Mountains of Maryland managed by the Seabees. President and Mrs. Reagan often invited a few White House staff members to accompany them and bring their families.

The business of the White House went on at Camp David. President Reagan worked on speeches, personally answered public mail, and on rare occasions hosted heads of state.

RANCHO DEL CIELO

Climb on the horse and virtually ride the hillside of Rancho del Cielo with the president in this gallery.

"The ranch was a sanctuary for us like none other."

- RONALD REAGAN

Rancho del Cielo was President and Mrs. Reagan's 688-acre ranch in the hills above Santa Barbara, California. They owned this property, featuring a modest 1,500-square-foot house, from 1974 to 1996. More than once President Reagan said that this was his favorite place on earth.

Reconnecting with nature inspired Ronald Reagan. Chores on the ranch such as clearing brush and repairing fences helped him to relax and keep fit. On rare occasions, illustrious visitors such as Queen Elizabeth and Mikhail Gorbachev were invited to join the Reagans at their rustic retreat.

"There's nothing better for the inside of a man than the outside of a horse."

- RONALD REAGAN

The old adobe ranch house that dates to 1872 was modest at best. The only heat was generated by two fireplaces. Ronald Reagan made improvements with his own hands to provide some comfort such as enclosing a patio to add room. The house was situated on a picturesque pond they named "Lake Lucky."

In a friendship that continued long after they left office, Ronald and Nancy Reagan hosted Mikhail and Raisa Gorbachev at their ranch on May 3, 1992.

"As I walk off… a final word to the men and women of the Reagan Revolution…
We did it. We weren't just marking time. We made a difference."

— RONALD REAGAN, FAREWELL ADDRESS TO THE NATION, JANUARY 11, 1989

After his years in the White House, Ronald Reagan continued to spread his lifelong message of freedom. He delivered talks in Great Britain, Japan, Poland, and the Soviet Union, among other nations.

Queen Elizabeth II conferred the Most Honorable Order of the Bath, the highest recognition Britain can give a foreigner, on President Ronald Reagan (right), on June 14, 1989.

> *"Whatever else history may say about me… I hope it will record that I appealed to your best hopes, not your worst fears; to your confidence, rather than your doubts."*
>
> — RONALD REAGAN, 1992

He made appearances at many events across the United States, from the Goodwill Games in Seattle, Washington, to Dwight Eisenhower's boyhood home in Abilene, Kansas. In 1992, Ronald Reagan stirred the Republican National Convention with his irrepressible patriotism and optimism: "Who among us," he asked, "would trade America's future for that of any other country in the world?"

RONALD REAGAN

Nov. 5, 1994

My Fellow Americans,

I have recently been told that I am one of the millions of Americans who will be afflicted with Alzheimer's Disease.

Upon learning this news, Nancy & I had to decide whether as private citizens we would keep this a private matter or whether we would make this news known in a public way.

In the past Nancy suffered from breast cancer and I had my cancer surgeries. We found through our open disclosures we were able to raise public awareness. We were happy that as a result many more people underwent testing. They were treated in early stages and able to return to normal, healthy lives.

So now, we feel it is important to share it with you. In opening our hearts, we hope this might promote greater awareness of this condition. Perhaps it will encourage a clearer understanding of the individuals and families who are affected by it.

At the moment I feel just fine. I intend to live the remainder of the years God gives me on this earth doing the things I have always done. I will continue to share life's journey with my beloved Nancy and my family. I plan to enjoy the great outdoors and stay in touch with my friends and supporters.

Unfortunately, as Alzheimer's Disease progresses, the family often bears a heavy burden. I only wish there was some way I could spare Nancy from this painful experience. When the time comes I am confident that with your help she will face it with faith and courage.

In closing, let me thank you, the American people for giving me the great honor of allowing me to serve as your President. When the Lord calls me home, whenever that may be, I will leave with the greatest love for this country of ours and eternal optimism for its future.

I now begin the journey that will lead me into the sunset of my life. I know that for America there will always be a bright dawn ahead.

Thank you my friends. May God always bless you.

Sincerely,
Ronald Reagan

On November 5, 1994, Ronald Reagan wrote this letter to the American people, revealing that he had been diagnosed with Alzheimer's disease. The onset of Alzheimer's disease ultimately robbed President Reagan of his greatest talents and ushered a celebrated statesman from the world stage.

> *"We have one beacon to guide us that Ronald Reagan never had. We have his example. Let us give thanks today for a life that achieved so much for all of God's children."*
>
> – MARGARET THATCHER, EULOGY FOR
> RONALD REAGAN, JUNE 11, 2004

Ronald Wilson Reagan died on Saturday, June 5, 2004, with his wife and family at his side. President George W. Bush declared June 11, 2004, a national day of mourning. People left flowers, American flags, and other symbols of their grief at U.S. embassies around the world, Ronald Reagan's birthplace, his college, and his presidential library. Condolences poured in from around the globe, from kings and queens as well as ordinary citizens.

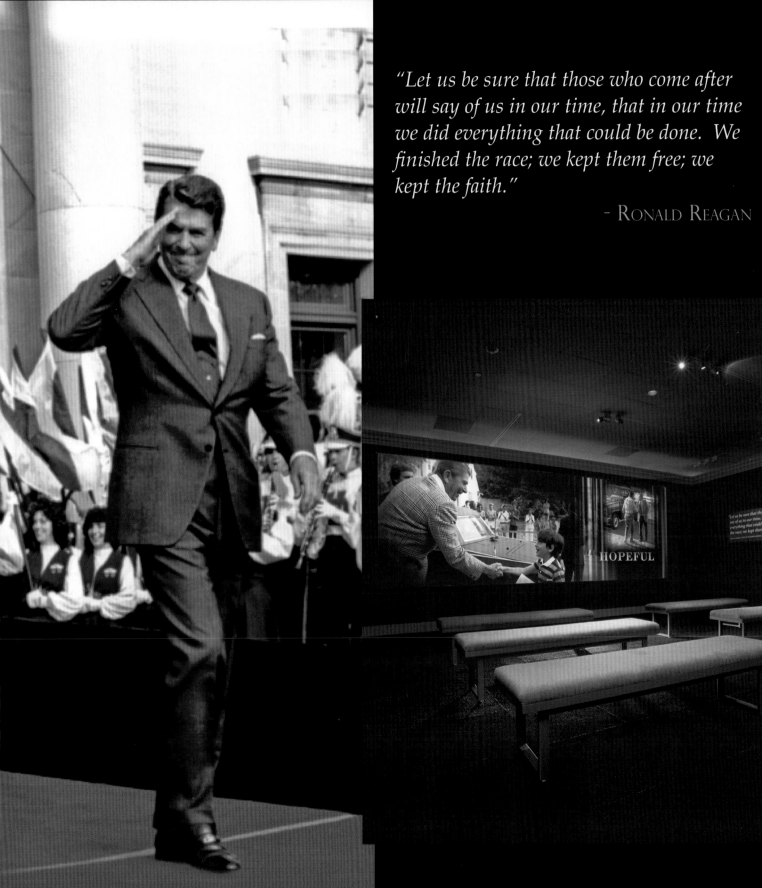

"Let us be sure that those who come after will say of us in our time, that in our time we did everything that could be done. We finished the race; we kept them free; we kept the faith."

- RONALD REAGAN

HOPEFUL

I KNOW IN MY HEART THAT MAN IS GOOD

THAT WHAT IS RIGHT WILL ALWAYS EVENTUALLY TRIUMPH

AND THERE IS PURPOSE AND WORTH TO EACH AND EVERY LIFE

RONALD WILSON REAGAN
FEBRUARY 6, 1911 – JUNE 5, 2004
NANCY DAVIS REAGAN
JULY 6, 1921 – MARCH 6, 2016

"I know in my heart that man is good, that what is right will always eventually triumph and there is purpose and worth to each and every life."

- RONALD REAGAN, NOVEMBER 4, 1991

Following his passing on June 5, 2004, at the age of ninety-three, President Ronald Wilson Reagan was laid to rest at the Reagan Library on June 11, 2004. He requested that his resting place be under an oak tree and facing the Pacific Ocean. President George W. Bush directed that every year, on Reagan's birth date of February 6, a military unit provide a twenty-one-gun salute and that a wreath be placed at the Memorial.

Captain James Symonds, Commanding Officer of the USS *Ronald Reagan*, presented the flag that draped President Reagan's casket to Mrs. Ronald Reagan.

On Friday, March 11, 2016, a military honor guard escorted the coffin of America's former first lady, Nancy Davis Reagan, to her final resting place next to her beloved husband at the Ronald Reagan Presidential Library. The Vicar of the National Cathedral quoted the poet, Van Dyke: "Time is too slow for those who wait, Too swift for those who fear, Too long for those who grieve, Too short for those who rejoice, But for those who love, Time is eternity."

On November 12, 2018, the Ronald Reagan Presidential Library and Museum installed a new Gold Star Families Memorial Monument to honor the families of the servicemen and women who sacrificed their lives while serving in the military.

The Ronald Reagan Presidential Library and Museum was dedicated on November 4, 1991. It has served thousands of researchers and millions of visitors, supported by the Ronald Reagan Presidential Foundation, the sole non-profit organization created to carry out President Reagan's work of inspiring freedom at home and abroad. Through the work of the Reagan Center for Public Affairs, the Walter and Leonore Annenberg Presidential Learning Center, the Discovery Center, and the Air Force One Pavilion, the Foundation continues his legacy and shares his principles: individual liberty, economic opportunity, global democracy, and national pride. Just as President Reagan would have it, his Foundation receives no government funding and relies solely on private donations for its support.

TIMELINE

1910s

February 6, 1911: Ronald Wilson Reagan is born in Tampico, Illinois

1913: The Reagan family moves to Chicago, the first of five moves in seven years

1920s

1920: The Reagan family settles in Dixon, Illinois

1924: Ronald Reagan enters Dixon High School

1926: Ronald Reagan begins the first of seven summers working as a lifeguard on the Rock River at Lowell Park, where he saved seventy-seven lives

1928: Ronald Reagan enters Eureka College and graduates in 1932

1930s

1932: Ronald Reagan lands a job in broadcasting at WOC in Davenport, Iowa

1937: Ronald Reagan moves to Hollywood after signing a seven-year contract with Warner Bros.

1940s

January 24, 1940: Ronald Reagan and actress Jane Wyman are married in Glendale, California

1940: Ronald Reagan appears in *Knute Rockne, All American*

January 4, 1941: Daughter Maureen Elizabeth Reagan is born in Los Angeles, California

1941: Jack Reagan, Ronald Reagan's father, dies of heart failure

1942: Ronald Reagan stars in the acclaimed *Kings Row*

April 1942: Second Lieutenant Ronald Reagan reports for active duty at Fort Mason, California, and is honorably discharged in 1945

March 18, 1945: Adopted son Michael Edward Reagan is born in Los Angeles, California

1946: Reagan returns to Hollywood and continues to make movies

1947: Ronald Reagan is elected to his first term as president of the Screen Actors Guild

1949: Ronald Reagan and Jane Wyman are divorced in Los Angeles, California

1950s

1950: Ronald Reagan meets actress Nancy Davis

March 4, 1952: Ronald Reagan marries Nancy Davis

October 21, 1952: Daughter Patricia Ann Reagan is born in Los Angeles, California

September 1954–1962: Ronald Reagan hosts *GE Theater* and becomes ambassador for the GE Corporation

May 28, 1958: Ronald Prescott Reagan is born in Los Angeles, California

1960s

1960: Ronald Reagan completes his fifth term as president of the Screen Actors Guild

1962: Nelle Reagan, Ronald Reagan's mother, dies in California of complications from Alzheimer's disease

October 27, 1964: Ronald Reagan delivers his landmark speech, "A Time for Choosing," on behalf of Barry Goldwater, the Republican nominee for president

1964: Ronald Reagan stars in his final movie, *The Killers*

1965: "Friends of Ronald Reagan" group is formed to support Ronald Reagan for governor of California in the 1966 election January 6, 1966: Ronald Reagan announces his intention to seek the Republican nomination for governor of the State of California

November 8, 1966: Ronald Reagan is elected governor of California

January 2, 1967: Ronald Reagan is sworn in as the thirty-third governor of California

August 1968: Governor Reagan enters the race for president of the United States as a "Favorite Son"

May 15, 1969: Governor Reagan sends the National Guard to the University of California, Berkeley to quell campus unrest

1970s

November 3, 1970: Governor Reagan elected to serve a second term

August 1971: Governor Reagan signs the California Welfare Reform Act into law, the most comprehensive initiative in American history

January 1975: Governor and Mrs. Reagan return to life as private citizens; Ronald Reagan delivers his first nationally syndicated weekly radio address

August 19, 1976: Ronald Reagan narrowly loses the Republican nomination for president to incumbent Gerald Ford

November 13, 1979: Ronald Reagan announces his candidacy for president of the United States

November 4, 1980: Ronald Reagan is elected the fortieth president of the United States

1980s

January 20, 1981: Ronald Reagan is inaugurated as the fortieth president of the United States; fifty-two American hostages are released from Iran

February 5, 1981: President Reagan addresses the nation on the economy

March 30, 1981: President Reagan is the victim of an assassination attempt

July 19–21, 1981: President Reagan participates in G-7 summits

August 3, 1981: Air traffic controllers strike; President Reagan orders controllers back to work within forty-eight hours

August 13, 1981: President Reagan signs the Economic Recovery Tax Act (ERTA)

September 25, 1981: Sandra Day O'Connor is sworn in as first female Supreme Court justice

January 26, 1982: President Reagan delivers his first State of the Union address

June 8, 1982: President Reagan delivers a speech to both houses of Parliament in the United Kingdom, announces that the "march of freedom and democracy will leave Marxism-Leninism on the ash-heap of history."

March 8, 1983: President Reagan calls the Soviet Union an "evil empire" in a landmark speech to the National Association of Evangelicals in Florida

March 23, 1983: President Reagan announces his Strategic Defense Initiative, an effort "which holds the promise of changing the course of human history."

April 18, 1983: Bombing of U.S. Embassy in Beirut, Lebanon; thirty-two killed

September 1, 1983: Soviet attack on Korean airliner KAL 007; 269 killed

October 23, 1983: Bombing of U.S. Marine barracks, Beirut, Lebanon; 241 U.S. marines, soldiers, and sailors killed

October 25, 1983: United States invades Grenada; rescues 1,000 U.S. citizens

November 6, 1984: President Reagan re-elected by a landslide

January 21, 1985: President Reagan inaugurated for a second term as president of the United States

November 16, 1985: President Reagan meets with Mikhail Gorbachev in Geneva, Switzerland, in the first of four major peace talks

January 28, 1986: Space shuttle Challenger explodes

October 11, 1986: President Reagan meets with Mikhail Gorbachev in Reykjavik, Iceland, in the second of four major summits

October 22, 1986: President Reagan signs the Tax Reform Act of 1986

1986–1987: The Iran-Contra controversy plagues the Reagan Administration

March 4, 1987: President Reagan addresses the nation on the Iran-Contra controversy

June 12, 1987: President Reagan gives his historic speech at the Berlin Wall, challenging Mikhail Gorbachev to "tear down this wall."

December 8, 1987: President Reagan meets with Mikhail Gorbachev in Washington, D.C., and together they sign the INF Treaty eliminating an entire class of nuclear weapons

June 1, 1988: INF Treaty is ratified in Moscow, U.S.S.R., by President Reagan and Mikhail Gorbachev

November 8, 1988: George Herbert Walker Bush is elected America's forty-first president

January 11, 1989: President Reagan gives his farewell address to the nation

January 20, 1989: President and Mrs. Reagan return to California

June 14, 1989: Queen Elizabeth II presents President Reagan with the Order of the Bath, the highest honorary knighthood of the British Orders of Chivalry

November 9, 1989: The Berlin Wall falls, reuniting Germany

1990s

June 4, 1990: President Reagan meets with General Secretary Gorbachev in San Francisco

September 1990: President Reagan addresses the shipyard workers in celebration of Solidarity in Gdansk, Poland

September 1990: President Reagan meets with Pope John Paul ll

February 4, 1991: President Reagan welcomes former British prime minister Margaret Thatcher to the Reagan Library

1991: The Soviet Union collapses, marking an end to the Cold War

November 4, 1991: The Ronald Reagan Presidential Library and Museum is dedicated and opens to the public

August 19, 1992: President Reagan addresses the Republican National Convention and says, "Whatever else history may say about me when I'm gone, I hope it will record that I appealed to your best hopes, not your worst fears; to your confidence, rather than your doubts. My dream is that you will travel the road ahead with liberty's lamp guiding your steps and opportunity's arm steadying your way"

January 13, 1993: President George H.W. Bush presents the Medal of Freedom to President Ronald Reagan at the White House

November 1994: Ronald Reagan composes a letter to the American people, disclosing his battle with Alzheimer's disease

2000s

August 8, 2001: Daughter Maureen Elizabeth Reagan dies of cancer at the age of sixty

June 5, 2004: At age ninety-three, Ronald Wilson Reagan dies of pneumonia, a complication of Alzheimer's, at the Reagans' Bel Air home in Los Angeles

June 7-8, 2004: Laid in Repose at the Ronald Reagan Presidential Library and Museum; over 120,000 people paid their respects

June 9-10, 2004: Laid in State in the Rotunda of the U.S. Capitol; over 100,000 people paid their respects

June 11, 2004: National funeral service is held at the Washington National Cathedral; final sunset service and interment at the Ronald Reagan Presidential Library and Museum

June 2, 2009: With Nancy Reagan present at the White House, President Barack Obama creates the Ronald Reagan Centennial Commission, an eleven-person panel to plan and carry out activities to mark the one-hundredth anniversary of the former presidents birth

2010s

February 6, 2011: Former First Lady Nancy Reagan presided over the Ronald Reagan Centennial Celebration, on what   would have been Ronald Reagan's 100th Birthday

September 7, 2011: Former First Lady Nancy Reagan hosted a national Republican Debate at the Ronald Reagan Presidential Library

September 16, 2015: Former First Lady Nancy Reagan hosted a national Republican Debate at the Ronald Reagan Presidential Library

March 6, 2016: Former First Lady Nancy Reagan, died at her home in Los Angeles, due to congestive heart failure, at the age of 94

March 11, 2016: Former First Lady Nancy Reagan was laid to rest next to her beloved husband at the Ronald Reagan Presidential Library

2020s

July 6, 2021-22: The Nancy Reagan Centennial is officially launched

June 7, 2022: The Ronald Reagan Institute in Washington, DC, is officially opened

The Ronald Reagan Presidential Library and Museum
40 Presidential Drive | Simi Valley, California 93065 | 800-410-8354
For more information, visit our website: www.reaganfoundation.org

Photographic Credits

The Ronald Reagan Presidential Foundation
John Martorano
Steve Whittaker
Ronald Reagan Presidential Library Collection

Copyright © 2011 by Ronald Reagan Presidential Library
Foundation. All right reserved.
Second Printing 2012
Third Printing 2014
Fourth Printing 2015
Fifth Printing 2017
Sixth Printing 2018

Library of Congress Cataloging Data

The Ronald Reagan Presidential Library and Museum.

ISBN 978-1-57864-673-9 (softcover : alk. paper)
1. Ronald Reagan Presidential Library and Museum. 2. Reagan, Ronald--Archives.
3. Presidents--United States--Archives. 4. Reagan, Ronald--Museums--California--Simi Valley.
5. Reagan, Ronald.6. Presidents--United States--Biography.
E838.5.R439R66 2011
027.5794'92--dc23
2011028267

Printed in the United States of America.